GUIDELINES
for Leading Your Congregation

CHURCH HISTORIAN

Remembering the past and inspiring the future

Written by

General Commission on Archives and History

CHURCH HISTORIAN

Copyright © 2000 by Cokesbury

This book is printed on elemental-chlorine–free paper.

ISBN 0-687-03551-1

MANUFACTURED IN THE UNITED STATES OF AMERICA

CONTENTS

Our Identity, Call, and Mission

About now a small voice in the back of your mind may be whispering, "What am I doing here? To what have I said yes? What is my role?" At the same time you may be aware that your congregation has extended to you a *call—a call to serve.* And you have said *yes—yes to leading in a vital mission.*

The mission of The United Methodist Church is to make disciples of Jesus Christ. You have agreed to serve as a leader bringing your unique passions, gifts, and abilities to the church. When the leaders focus on the church's purpose—*its mission of making disciples of Jesus Christ*—and link that purpose to the passions of the people, amazing things can happen.

The fundamental __way__ we fulfill our mission is to reach out to people in the name of Jesus Christ, to relate people to God, to nurture and strengthen them in their journey of discipleship, and to send them into the world to be the church— inviting and receiving others in the name of Jesus Christ. We call this the primary task of The United Methodist Church. Effective leaders keep the whole of the primary task in their sight, working to keep all of its aspects in concert.

Leaders in the church must be first, and foremost, spiritual leaders who model and embrace Christian discipline and teaching. *By practicing the means of grace*—prayer, fasting, studying Scripture, corporate worship, celebration of the Lord's Supper, Christian conversation, and acts of mercy—*church leaders stay tuned to the mission of the church and live out the primary task.* Members and would-be members should be able to look to a congregation's leaders for spiritual example and direction, because true leaders are known by their fruits. People's lives are changed through their influence.

Leaders use their gifts and talents to enable others to use __their__ gifts and talents to the fullest potential. The flow of information, inspiration, guidance, and vision from leaders is an encouragement to others on their spiritual journey. Leaders help others to see new possibilities. When leaders are focused on the mission of the church, community is built and ministry occurs. The church focused on God is alive with creative energy aimed at transformation.

Four Essential Leadership Functions

Church leaders support and strengthen the church when they pay attention to these leadership functions: (1) help people discover the current reality in which they live; (2) bring together the congregation's understandings of __current__ reality and __desired__ reality into a shared vision; (3) develop the plans to help the community move from current reality toward the reality of its shared vision; and finally, (4) monitor the whole work of the church as the congregation moves with God's guidance toward its vision.

1. Discovering Current Reality

Accurately describing current reality—the way things are—may be the most important function of leadership. The booklets in this Guideline series offer suggestions for leaders to pay attention to the various committees of the church's ministry. In addition, it is critical for church leaders—lay and clergy—to spend time together discussing the ministry of the whole congregation. The conversation needs to include attentiveness to God's guidance and everything that describes a congregation's "what we are, here and now." Because God is always doing a new thing, this job is continuous. When we pay attention to change, we provide a base of integrity and strength from which to move into the future. Faith in Jesus Christ and a spiritual centering in God offers the strongest foundation to move people fearlessly through the massive changes of the twenty-first century.

2. Naming Shared Vision

Ask the question, "What do you want more than anything else in the world?" and most persons will give a response that indicates that they want to live in a world filled with love, faith, security, and meaning. Because persons desire a positive future, they are willing to invest themselves in organizations that are committed to it. By its very nature, the church is devoted to the creation of a better future. When the church promises to move people personally and corporately toward their desired reality, people will invest time, energy, and resources into the church. As people see their own desires linked to the congregational vision and deeper understanding of God's future, they deepen their commitment and involvement. Building this link is a vital role of leadership.

Naming a shared vision is accomplished by asking people about their lives and their faith, and listening very carefully. By listening, we mean deep listening— the kind that requires setting aside our own agendas and entering into the worldviews of others, and listening for God through the conversation. It is a significant shift in our understanding of leadership in the church to move from telling people what we think they need to know to listening to people in order to find out who they are and what their desired realities are. Effective spiritual leaders listen to the hearts of people and begin to articulate a shared vision.

3. Developing Bridges

To span the gulf between our current reality and the hope expressed in the shared vision, leaders must build a bridge. The third critical function of leadership is to plan actions and develop systems that create the bridge across this gulf. Leaders who are elected to administrative and program committees are responsible for the ongoing work of the church and must pay attention to the present. At the same time, leaders *must* be focused on the future—keeping today and tomorrow in tension—ensuring that the church doesn't get stuck in the past, present, or future.

Church leaders who are attentive to God's leading and who can hold the tension between today and tomorrow are *visionary leaders*. Visionary leaders see it all—current reality, desired reality, and the bridges to get from one to the other.

4. Monitoring the Journey

Perhaps the most critical task for leaders is keeping an eye on the whole of the faith journey of the congregation. When leaders are constantly caught up in "doing" the administrative and program work of the church, there is not any time left for "being" with God in prayer to discern the leading of the Spirit for the congregation. Leaders must step back from "doing" constant activities in order to pay attention to the total direction of the church's mission and ministry. All elected and appointed leaders must spend time together listening to God in prayer, Bible study, conversation, and other means of grace in order to lead the entire community in the work of Christ. Anything less is not Christian spiritual leadership.

Using This Guideline

This Guideline is designed to help you, the local church historian, in your ministry. It also serves as a companion to the video *Memory and Ministry: Caring for Your Church's Heritage,* which offers specific training in the collection, arrangement, preservation, and interpretation of local church records. The video is available from Ecufilm, 810 Twelfth Avenue, South, Nashville, TN 37203; 800-251-4091.

This Is Your Job

Your basic responsibilities as local church historian are described in ¶ 246.5a of *The Book of Discipline.* Work with your pastor(s) and church staff, the Committee on Records and History (if one exists), and lay leadership to design procedures that will help you fulfill your disciplinary duties.

As historian, you will want to:

• Establish an archives if one does not already exist.
• Encourage church officers to keep accurate church records.
• Provide for the preservation of all records and historical materials no longer in current use.
• Promote interest in the history and heritage of The United Methodist Church and of your own congregation.
• Assist the pastor and others in the annual observance of Heritage Sunday and in the celebration of significant anniversaries.
• Serve as a member of the Committee on Records and History if one exists.
• Serve on the church council and/or other committees to which the local church historian is assigned.
• Help those who wish to do research in your church's records.

These are the basics. Don't be afraid to branch out, though! Work with your pastor and other church leaders to identify the places and times where you can use your God-given abilities and interests to serve the church in the ministry of history. You may have special gifts in writing, drama, music, working with children, or public relations. Use them to make history come alive! Design a job description and set work goals that include your basic responsibilities, but that also suit you and your abilities. Circulate it to the church leadership so that everyone knows that the church historian is an active, vital part of the church's ministry.

The historian's job is a demanding one if it is done well. If the church does not already have a Committee on Records and History, it might be wise to establish one so that others can share the responsibilities. See *The Book of Discipline* for guidance.

Other persons and organizations are ready to help you. Among them are your annual conference Commission on Archives and History, the General Commission on Archives and History, state and local libraries and historical societies, and other local church historians in your area. Don't hesitate to ask for their assistance. If they cannot help you, they will be able to recommend someone who can. (See Resources for more information.)

The Ministry of History
Why does history matter?

One of the chief values of history is *entertainment*. It is fascinating to learn about the people of the past. We enjoy listening, seeing, and reading about what has happened in the past. Many in your congregation will be captivated by the stories of people and events in your church's history.

History can also be a source of *inspiration*. As we learn more about those who created the heritage of which we are heirs, we may be inspired to give thanks for their lives, and we may pledge to follow their example. On the other hand, we recognize that history is made by people who are not always at their best, and their stories may evoke our confession of their shortcomings and inspire us to say that we shall learn from their mistakes.

Finally, we know that history's real importance is that it helps us in *understanding who we are*. It is a clue to our own identity. Your church's present-day location, its architecture, its worship style, its organization, its ministries and outreach, and countless other facets of its life are all rooted in the history of the congregation. By reflecting on the past, we can better understand who we are and determine the future directions of our ministry.

History is ministry! Your job is an important part of the church's ministry as you help it record and remember its service for Christ.

What Are Archives?

Have you ever noticed how often we use the same word in a variety of ways? Just think of the different meanings of the term *annual conference*. The word *archives* is like that, too. *Archives* can refer to a storage place for historically important records. But *archives* can also refer to the records themselves. In this section we describe just what we mean by historical records and other terms used in this guideline.

Accession: When records are added to an archives, the transaction is called an accession.

Accession list/register: A simple form listing each accession, the date it was received, and the name of the person(s) or office who gave the materials.

Acid-free paper: Paper having a pH of 7.0 or greater. It is commonly available in stationery stores.

Acquisition policy: Every archival depository must decide which materials it will and will not add to its collection. An acquisition policy briefly summarizes that information.

Administrative value: Records have administrative or operational value when they are needed by an office, an organization, or a person in order to conduct business now and in the future.

Archives: (1) The documents created or received and accumulated by a person or organization in the course of the conduct of affairs and preserved because of their continuing value. (2) The building or part of a building where archival materials are located; can also be called an archival repository.

Archives box/container: A container that stores and protects various types of archival materials. It is often called a Hollinger box after a prominent manufacturer.

Arrangement: The process of sorting, organizing, and shelving records so that they can be readily retrieved and used.

Collection: (1) The total group of records created by a person, an institution, or an organization. (2) The total holdings of an archival repository.

Correspondence: Any form of addressed and written communication sent and received, including letters, postcards, memoranda, and notes.

Current records: Records that should stay in office files because they are needed to conduct current business.

Deed of gift: A contract establishing conditions governing the transfer of title to documents and specifying any restrictions on access or use. They are signed by the donor and by a person representing the repository.

Description: The process of describing archival holdings so that researchers can easily understand their contents.

Document: Information recorded in any format, from paper to computer disk.

Donor: Someone (a person, group, or institution) that gives materials to an archival repository.

Encapsulation: Placing a paper document in a clear plastic envelope (usually polyester) and sealing the edges with special tape. This supports and protects fragile items, but still allows them to be viewed and handled.

Evidential value: Records have evidential value when they provide evidence of a person's, organization's, or institution's origins, functions, and activities.

File: A group of documents grouped in a folder or a volume.

Files: All or part of the records of an office or agency.

Finding aid: A document that specifically describes all or part of an archives' holdings. It is usually designed to be used by interested persons to locate information in the archives.

Guide: A document that describes all or part of an archives' holdings. It is not as specific as a finding aid.

Holdings: All of the materials held by an archival repository.

Hollinger box: see Archives box/container.

Inactive records: see Noncurrent records.

Informational value: Documents have informational value when they contain helpful and interesting data. This is distinct from any evidential value they may have.

Manuscript: A handwritten or typed document.

Minutes: Memoranda or notes of a proceeding.

Noncurrent records: Records no longer needed to conduct current business.

Personal papers: The documents belonging to an individual.

Processing: The activities of caring for records: adding them to the archives (accession), organizing them (arrangement and description), preparing finding aids, and properly storing them.

Record: A document created by or for a person, organization, or institution.

Records center: A place where semicurrent records are stored until decisions are made about their ultimate disposition.

Records center carton/container: A specially designed corrugated cardboard box.

Repository: A place where archives are housed; also called a depository.

Semicurrent records: Records that are needed occasionally by an office or a person.

Stacks: The shelved storage area in a library or archives repository.

Putting the Pieces Together

Step 1: Survey the Church's Records

The history of your church is like a big jigsaw puzzle. The puzzle pieces are the documents and other materials that have recorded your church's story since its founding. The following steps will help you put the pieces together.

How do you create a good church archives? First, discover what you already have. If your church does not have an archives or historical room, then start with a survey. Just as the pioneers of the past went out into the wilderness to survey unknown lands, you must journey through your church to discover where its records are kept.

Before you begin the actual survey, create a list of the various groups in your church. Such a list can be found in your charge conference reports. (You may know of another place where such a list exists.) Identify the groups that create the records in your church, such as the charge conference, or church council and its various committees.

Records are also created by Sunday school classes, youth groups, United Methodist Women and United Methodist Men, and other fellowship groups. Special occasions leave records (daily vacation Bible school, a missions outreach project, or a centennial celebration). Be as comprehensive as you can. If your church is the result of a merger, then remember to include any groups that were in the predecessor congregations.

Now you are ready to survey the church's records. Some records, of course, will be in the office of the church secretary, the church administrator, or the financial officer, not to mention the pastor's office. Records may be in desks, closets, or bookcases; under staircases and behind doors; in the attic or the boiler room; in Sunday school classrooms or the custodian's office.

Let people know what you are doing before you begin. Work with the pastor and church staff to examine the records on hand in the church office. With the staff's cooperation, explore other offices and rooms of the church.

Make a list of the records you find, noting their dates, condition, and location. This list does not have to be fancy. It is a tool to help you discover what you have in your church and where it is located. A little later we will talk about bringing the material together and arranging it.

Locating Missing Records

After you complete the list, organize the information so that you can determine what records may be missing.

You may find, for instance, that you have financial ledgers for every decade but the 1940s; that you could locate only one Women's Society minute book; and that membership records are complete from the date the church was founded to the present time.

Your next task is to discover what records may be in the hands of church members. This can be a delicate assignment, for persons often feel a real sense of ownership of church records and believe that they will take better care of them than the church historian. You will be most successful when you (with the pastor's help) can communicate a feeling of shared responsibility and stewardship to the congregation. It is important to stress that the church's records tell the story of the whole church family and belong where everyone can have access to them.

One way to approach the task is to make a list of records that you know are missing. Circulate the list among the congregation, former officials, pastors who have moved away, and children of deceased members. Invite their cooperation in collecting missing records.

Consider launching your campaign with a Homecoming Heritage Sunday. Church families can bring records, scrapbooks, photographs, and memorabilia to display. Provide space for each family to show and share. Ask each participant to make a list of what he or she brought so that you can have the information for reference. This is the time to begin talking to persons about transferring church records to your care.

Contact your annual conference Commission on Archives and History to determine whether any church records have been deposited at your conference archives. If you are unsure about whom to contact, check the most recent conference journal in the church office. The conference archives contains other sources of information about your church, including conference journals and newspapers.

Records may have found their way to a local public library or historical society. In addition, it will be helpful for you to survey local and regional newspapers from the years since your church's founding. There you will find descriptions of the church's programs; articles about members; birth, wedding, and funeral reports; and feature stories about special church events. Photocopies of this valuable information will enrich your church's archives.

Occasionally, someone will want to donate personal belongings to the archives. If you wish to accept such a gift, you will find it helpful to have a donor agreement form (approved by the charge conference). Having this form avoids future confusion over the ownership of the items. Your local historical society or library may have a donor form that you can use as a model, or you can use the language suggested below:

I, *(donor name),* own the items described below. I do hereby give and deliver the property described below to the *(name of church).* I understand that, unless excepted below, I am giving *(name of church)* full ownership of this property, including copyright and without limitation in the right to reproduce, adapt, publish, perform, or publicly display the property. Any part of the property that is not retained by *(name of church)* should be *(select one of the following)* returned to me, disposed of by the church, other *(explain).*

The agreement should be signed and dated by the church historian and the donor. Keep a copy of the agreement, and provide a copy for the donor along with an expression of appreciation.

Type of Records	Dates	Condition	Location
Women's Society minute book	1877–1893	water damage/mildew	box in broom closet
Financial ledger	1970s?	excellent	church office
25 loose photographs	unknown	no identification	Christian education office
Original deed to the church	1873	framed	in the pastor's study

Step 2: Understand What to Keep and What to Throw Away

One of the biggest challenges of caring for church records is knowing what should be kept and what should be discarded. Many questions will arise as you survey the materials in the church, as persons give you items for the archives, and as you collect minutes, reports, and other materials from church committees and organizations. The first question is, What should I keep? The answer can be complicated, for there is not a hard-and-fast rule that applies to all churches.

Some of your decisions about what to keep will be based on factors you cannot control. The size of your church, both in membership and in its physical plant, will affect your ability to retain the records of your past. If your storage area is very small, you will be able to save only the most vital records. If your church has saved very few records from the past, virtually everything you can find is a valuable record. On the other hand, if you are fortunate enough to have an abundance of records, you can afford to be a little more selective about what you will keep.

As painful as it is to say, there is generally not enough room to save all we would like to save, so it is necessary to make some decisions about what to keep. Below is a table that lists some of the most significant items to preserve. This table is meant to be a guideline.

Some records should be kept for a few years, but then may be discarded. These records help the church do its business efficiently and usually include financial records such as canceled checks, invoices, and records of giving.

Certain financial records may need to be kept permanently, depending on the laws in your town, city, or state. In most cases the majority of your financial records do not need to be kept for historical reasons. But be sure to check with your church legal counsel or financial officer before throwing those records away. If you determine that such records do not have historical value, notify the appropriate person(s) so that the records can be destroyed when they are no longer needed.

Other materials may be kept if you find them of historical interest and have room for them, but these are not vital documents and may be discarded. In this category are office calendars, office memos, budget work sheets, and general correspondence. These can be thrown away when they no longer serve any useful purpose in your church office. Once a year, for example, the church secretary can dispose of general correspondence that is at least one year old. (However, you may want to keep correspondence that documents some special function of your church, such as a particular service to the community.)

In doing your survey, you may have discovered that you have multiple copies of some items. People may also give you copies of material you already have. You can ask that the church approve the policy that no more than two of the same item be kept. Doing that will ensure wise and efficient use of your space, which is always limited.

Finally, before you throw materials away, consider whether they might be of interest to another archives or library. For example, it is not necessary to save local newspapers in your church archives, but your town or county historical society may be very interested in adding them to its collection.

Keep These Records!

Description	
Administrative reports	Permanent
Charge conference reports, administrative board reports, council on ministries report, or church council reports	Permanent
Architectural drawings, blueprints, maps, legal documents, and deeds	Permanent
Annual budget	Permanent
Sunday worship bulletins and bulletins printed for special occasions	Permanent
Local church committee records	Permanent

Directories	Permanent
Membership registers, baptisms, marriages, transfers	Permanent
Church newsletters, UMW, UMM, UMYF, and other church group newsletters	Permanent
Scrapbooks, photographs, mementos of special occasions	Permanent

Step 3: Organize Your Records

The next step in creating your archives is organizing and arranging the records that you located in your survey (Step 1) and decided to keep (Step 2). This third step is important so that you and others can have easy access to the church's records (and therefore its memory).

The two lists you created in Step 1 will come in handy now. They are, first, the list of the groups and organizations in your local church and, second, the list noting what records you located and where they currently may be found in the church. Now is the time to physically bring those records together in one place and to arrange them.

This presupposes that you will have someplace to put the records once you have arranged them. (See "Step 4: Care for Your Records" for information about the appropriate kind of space to store records.)

"Like goes with like" is the best rule for arranging your records. Using the list of groups in your church as a guide, sort the materials by their connection to those groups.

1. Assemble all the records of a particular group. For example, if you found administrative board minutes in the basement, attic, and the pastor's closet, put all of those records together. Do the same for all the other groups.
2. Then sort each group by record type. For example, the administrative board group may include minutes, reports, and long-range plans. Place all the minutes together in chronological order. Do the same for reports and then the long-range plans. A Sunday school group might have a class newsletter and photographs from various events. Sort the newsletters by date and then the photographs.
3. Sort some records, such as correspondence files, alphabetically. Even though you can often sort records by their dates, it is not always the correct way to arrange materials.

Here is how the arrangement may look when you are finished:

Administrative Board
    Minutes
        January-June 1969
        July-December 1969
        January-June 1970
        (and so on)

    Reports
        November 1969

November 1970
(and so on)
Sunday morning worship bulletins
    1915–1930
    1934–present

As the list illustrates, you do not need to note every individual item. You can think of each line as representing a file folder. Some folders may have several items in them (such as the bulletins or the administrative board minutes), while others may contain only a single item (such as the administrative board reports). The point is to place the groups in proper, or reasonable, order and to place the items in a file folder so that the folder is of manageable size.

4. On each file folder write (in pencil) the name of the group (such as "Administrative Board") and the type of record (such as "minutes") and the dates covered by the material in the file folder. Note the same information on a separate list.
5. If your local church is the result of a merger of other churches and if you have their records, as you should, keep those records separate. In this case the arrangement is a little more complicated. For example, we can imagine the case of two churches, St. Luke's and St. John's, which merged into a third, St. Paul's. Your arrangement should reflect each predecessor church, so you would create a list titled "St. Luke's" in which you would identify all the records related to that church. You would repeat the process for St. John's and for St. Paul's. The arrangement might look something like this:

St. Luke's
Administrative Board
    Minutes
            January-June 1869
            July-December 1869
            January-June 1870
            (and so on)
    Reports
            November 1869
            November 1870
            (and so on)

Sunday morning worship bulletins
            1865–1880
St. John's
Administrative Board
    Minutes
            January-June 1879
            July-December 1879
            January-June 1880
            (and so on)

Reports
>November 1879
>November 1880
>(and so on)

Sunday morning worship bulletins
>1885–1888

St. Paul's
a list of its records as above

6. Consider one final note on arrangement. If your church is old enough, and it probably is, you will notice that some organizations have gone through several name changes. For example, the Woman's Society of Christian Service and the Wesleyan Service Guild were names of groups that later became United Methodist Women; the Fourth Quarterly Conference became the charge conference and the board of stewards was followed by the board of trustees. What should be done about these name changes and reorganizations? The easiest method is to arrange all the groups alphabetically, no matter when they existed. This is the simplest approach by far and the recommended one in most cases. But it does require you to remember the connections between groups as they change names, and split apart.

The other possibility is to arrange the material by functions within the local church. Within the function group you can arrange the material chronologically. The following function groups are suggested: Administrative, Sunday Schools, Women, Men, and Youth. Underneath each function you can then place the groups that dealt with similar concerns. A broad outline could look like this:

Administrative
>Board of Stewards
>>list of records
>Board of Trustees
>>list of records
>Administrative Board
>>list of records

Women
>Woman's Society of Christian Service
>>list of records
>Wesleyan Service Guild
>>list of records
>United Methodist Women
>>list of records

This approach can be useful if you have many records from each predecessor group or if you have very few records from the predecessor groups and don't want them to get lost in the organization. Your church (or a church that merged with yours) may have belonged to one of the denominations that predates The United Methodist Church. The following information will help you sort out the records that belong to each denomination:

The United Methodist Church and Its Predecessors

Methodist Episcopal Church (1784–1939)

Methodist Episcopal Church, South (1844–1939)

Methodist Protestant Church (1830–1939)

The Methodist Church (1939–1968)

Church of the United Brethren in Christ (1800–1946)

Evangelical Association (1803–1922)

United Evangelical Church (1894–1922)

Evangelical Church (1922–1946)

Evangelical United Brethren Church (1946–1968)

The United Methodist Church (1968–present)

Step 4: Care for Your Records

Here are some ways to prolong the life of your church's records:

1. Unfold all documents to their full size for permanent storage. Folded papers will eventually tear at the fold. You may need to provide a special storage area for oversized material.
2. Remove rubber bands, which deteriorate over time and adhere to documents. Also remove paper clips, staples, and other fasteners. Metal fasteners can rust. They also catch and cause tears as you remove documents from folders.
3. Place your records in acid-free file folders, and store them in acid-free containers, which are specially designed to protect your documents. See pages 30-31 for a list of suppliers.
4. Make photocopies on acid-free paper of newspaper clippings you wish to save. This can be done for any item that has important information printed on poor quality paper. See pages 30-31 for a list of suppliers.
5. Place fragile documents in Mylar or polyethylene covers, which will provide additional support to the paper when handling is necessary. See pages 30-31 for a list of suppliers.
6. Learn how to encapsulate documents. Doing this will give greater protection to some of your older records. Don't confuse this with lamination, which should be avoided. Regional and local historical societies or libraries should be able to assist you.
7. Store photographs and negatives in isolation from other materials. They can be stored singly in acid-free, Mylar, or polyethylene envelopes, or collectively in a folder as long as a piece of acid-free paper is placed between each image. It is best to write all identifying information either on the envelope or in the front or back margin of the photograph. Pens especially designed for this purpose are available. See pages 30-31 for a list of suppliers.
8. Do not write on or mark the papers in your custody. Be sure that persons using the archives do not underline or mark the documents in any way.
9. If papers become water-soaked, move them to a dry storage area. Place an

electric fan in the area and dry at normal temperatures. The fan is necessary to create moving air. Mold is more likely to grow if the air is still.

10. If there is evidence of bugs or vermin in your archives, have the area fumigated. Check over your records carefully to see if there is any infestation in the boxes. If so, isolate the boxes with appropriate bug traps.

11. Use only archival mending tape when making minor repairs.

12. Follow these procedures to create a permanent record:
    • Use a permanent black ink pen to take handwritten minutes and other local church records.
    • Use acid-free paper for all of your permanent records, such as reports and minutes.
    • Create scrapbooks with acid-free materials only.
    • Attach scrapbook items in such a way that the items can be removed without damage either to themselves or to the scrapbook pages. Use corner holders, water-soluble glue, or Mylar sheets. Avoid cellophane and transparent tapes, which will discolor with age, shrink, become brittle, and eventually detach, leaving ugly and damaging yellow stains on the material.

13. Treat the contents of cornerstone boxes with special care. Careless or improper handling of the box itself may damage the items inside. Arrange to copy the contents immediately after opening the box. Avoid using cornerstones in the future. They do not protect the items well. If your church wants to preserve something for future members to look at, invest the time and funds into a church archives/history room.

14. Always feel free to ask for help or advice. Contact local historical societies, your annual conference Commission on Archives and History, or the General Commission on Archives and History if you have questions.

15. Having taken the time to protect your records by placing them in the proper containers, think about the type of room in which to store them.
    • The storage room should be cool and dry. If nothing else, a relatively constant temperature and humidity will help preserve your records. Avoid placing your archives in either the attic or the basement. A temperature between 65 degrees and 70 degrees Fahrenheit, with around 48 percent relative humidity, is ideal.
    • Storing the items and boxes on steel shelving is better than on wood. Most wood has been treated in a manner similar to standard boxes and file folders. Given time, the wood will damage your storage containers.
    • Your items will be more secure if the storage area can be locked and only a limited number of people have access to the keys.
    • If possible, your records should be kept in a fireproof or fire-resistant room or storage area.
    • Your storage area should have smoke alarms wired into your general alarm system for the entire church.
    • You are wise to keep a fire extinguisher handy, preferably two: one for paper fires and another for electrical fires.

Step 5: Manage the Records

If we are to have a past for the future, we must preserve the records of today. This is the function of records management.

A records management program strives to achieve economy and efficiency in the creation, use, maintenance, and disposal of church records.

Effective use of space and time. After personnel costs, records keeping is one of the largest administrative expenditures in the church. Record creation, maintenance, filing, office storage space, filing supplies, and equipment all contribute to the high cost of keeping records.

Legal protection. If your church is ever faced with legal action, having a records management program in place can assure courts and litigants that records are being disposed of properly and in a routine manner, not maliciously or capriciously.

Records management is the attempt to systematically control the growth and disposition, or destruction, of your records. Its basic purpose is to help answer those nagging questions, What do I keep? How long do I keep it? and When can I remove it from my office?

Now we need to define some terms. In every office a variety of records are related because they result from the same filing process, or the same function, or the same activity, or have a similar form or content. This group of related documents is called a *series.* For example, file folders of bank statements from different banks are a series, as are a collection of invoices or of staff memos. For each series there are two important questions to be asked. The first is, How are these records used?—this is referred to as the *records life cycle.* The second is, How significant are these records?—this is referred to as *appraisal.*

Records Life Cycle
Records are almost living organisms. They are born, mature during their use, and then are retired or removed. In records management the task is to recognize when a record has reached the end of its life cycle or no longer serves a useful administrative function. In general, the less a record is consulted, the less useful it is administratively. When a record has reached the end of its useful administrative function, it is ready to be retired from the office. The function of *appraisal* helps us determine when to retire the record and what to do with the record once it is retired.

Records Appraisal
Appraisal is the process by which we determine the administrative, legal, and fiscal value (primary value) and the historical and long-term research value (secondary value) of records. Once the value of a record series has been determined, a realistic retention period can be assigned to it. Appraisal can take place at any point during a record series' life cycle, but it is most frequently done when the records become inactive.

There are several questions to be asked when appraising a series: How frequently is the record used by those who created it? If the record is still frequently consulted, then it should probably remain in the office. If the record is not consulted frequently, is there still a consistent, although low, demand for it? Is there a legal or fiscal need to hold on to the record even though it is no longer consulted or used? An example is financial information. What is the historical significance of the record? By and large, records with historical significance provide information about the church, such as charge conference records or administrative board minutes.

Records management is something that can be handled at the local church level. You can do it with the help of your church's legal counsel, your annual conference Commission on Archives and History, and the General Commission on Archives and History. The General Commission on Archives and History (GCAH) has published a set of guidelines that can help your local church establish its own retention schedules. (Contact GCAH for more information.) A reasonable program can be set up so that what needs to be saved for the archives will be saved and what needs to be protected for the successful administration of your church's ministry will be preserved.

Step 6: Tell Your Church's Story to the Future

We create history every day of our lives, as individuals and as church congregations. Yesterday's worship service or committee meeting is today's history. Part of your responsibility as church historian is to document the unfolding story of your church.

One way to approach the task of saving today's history is to ask yourself what you would like to know about your church's past. Are those kinds of stories and records from today being preserved now for tomorrow? Imagine your church a century from now trying to discover what the congregation was like in the 1990s and early 2000s. How did we worship? What social issues most concerned us? What were our mission and evangelism outreaches? What was Sunday school like? What music did we sing? Who were the people active in our church's life and ministry? How did we have fun?

You know that your church's history is more than the names of its pastors and the dates when new buildings were constructed. The story of the church is the story of the whole congregation: pastors, Sunday school teachers, choirs, youth groups, mission circles, men, women, and children. Your challenge is to collect those records and artifacts that will help tell an inclusive, three-dimensional story of today's church for tomorrow's researcher.

Your own enthusiasm for the task of locating local church history sources will spark enthusiasm in others. Your most valuable resource may be a network of persons who care as you do about recovering local church history.

Establish a good working relationship with the key leaders who are making history, especially the pastor(s) and other staff members. Work with the church secretary and the secretaries of committees and organizations so that they will understand what materials are important to save.

Besides ensuring that essential church records are kept properly, what are some ways that you can document the less formal parts of current church life? How much material you can collect will depend in large part on the amount of storage space you have and (even more important) on your level of energy and enthusiasm, but here are some ways to document your church's ministry today:

• Ask persons to give you newspaper clippings with references to church members. Photocopy them, and keep them in a human interest file.
• Videotape a typical Sunday morning worship service.
• Enlist an enthusiastic photographer to shoot a week in the life of the church, covering everything from worship to committee meetings, choir practice to Mom's Day Out. Make sure that all photos are identified!
• Ask Sunday school classes of children, youth, and adults to respond in writing to the question, "I like our church because . . . ," to capture a sense of the congregation's personality.
• Invite the youth group to create a video tour of the church and its programs. Not only will you document the daily life of the church, but you'll get a good idea of what today's young people think is important.
• Do an oral history project (see pages 21-24).

Preserving contemporary history is a special challenge in two particular kinds of churches. The first is the congregation that believes its history is all in the past. The other is the new congregation, started in the last fifty years, where there are still members who can remember the beginning. We can easily become careless about documenting our history when the church's whole lifetime is within living memory. However, even the newest congregation has a need to preserve its history in more permanent forms than human memory.

Whether your church is new or old, struggling or thriving, the story of its people and its ministry should be preserved for future generations. The record of what God has wrought through your local church is worthy of being saved. God is alive and working in congregations, young and old, large and small, rural and urban. The story must be recorded and shared. Let us be responsible for sharing the tradition with future generations.

Doing Oral History

As you read through your church's records, do you wish you could ask, What was it really like? Dry statistics and bland reports suddenly come to life when we hear the personal stories of the people involved. Those stories from long ago are lost to us, but with an oral history project, it is possible to preserve today's stories for the future.

In the past, we could rely only on the written word for records. Today, with audiotape and videotape, we can record people's memories in their own voices, with the shading, nuance, and emphasis that give language its emotion and richness. Oral history interviews record eyewitness accounts of important events, significant persons, trends, changes, and continuity in the life of your church. The memories of church members add detail and dimension to the basic facts recorded in documents.

Before You Begin

An oral history project takes time, careful planning, and commitment. Before you begin, ask yourself what you want the project to accomplish. Will you focus on gathering the stories of your older members? Will the emphasis be on a particular era (such as World War II) or on a crucial event in the life of the church (such as its involvement in a particular mission)? Do you want this to be an intergenerational experience, comparing perceptions and experiences of different age groups?

As you define the project, create a list of persons (narrators) you would like to interview. The church staff and other congregational leaders may also be able to offer suggestions. Invite each narrator well ahead of time, and describe the project carefully. You may even want to write out a page of information for your narrators so that they know what is expected of them. It is good policy to prepare a statement for both the interviewer and the narrator to sign that will permit others to use the information gathered in the interview. This will help the narrator understand that the interview will become part of the church's records.

Develop a realistic schedule for the interviews. You will be exhausted if you try to do twenty-five interviews in a two-week period! Pace yourself so that your own enthusiasm and interest remain high. Each interview should feel fresh, even if you have asked some of the questions a dozen times before.

Make sure you are comfortable with your equipment before you begin. The narrator will relax and speak more naturally if the tape recorder or video camera is unobtrusive.

What Do You Want to Know?
Remember that the interview should not simply record information available elsewhere. Rather, it should supplement and clarify written records. The direction of the interview will depend in part on your goals for the oral history project and in part on the personality and experiences of the narrator. One or two casual conversations with the narrator in the days and weeks leading up to the interview will help you determine what subject areas you can cover.

Come to the interview with a list of subject areas and tentative questions. These will help you direct the interview. The subject areas you cover will reflect the narrator's personal history as well as the oral history project's focus, but general areas will be of interest in all but the most tightly focused interviews. These include the following:

• The narrator's family background
• How he or she first became involved with your church
• Earliest memories of church participation
• Descriptions of worship experiences
• Memories of major events in the life of the church
• Reminiscences of people
• Descriptions of the community in different eras
• Opinions on matters that have had a major impact on the church
• The narrator's feelings and thoughts about the church today

Getting It All on Tape
Your task as the interviewer is to encourage the narrator to tell his or her story. You should guide the narrator with brief questions, but this is not the place for you to share your own memories.

Start the interview with background questions, such as where the narrator was born, when he or she joined the church, and basic family information. This will help both you and the narrator become comfortable with the interview process.

After establishing basic facts, it is time to move into the body of the interview. Use the list of subject areas and tentative questions that you prepared earlier. You will need to be both firm and flexible. It is important not to let the interview stray too far into subjects that are not really relevant, but it is also important to allow the narrator to talk about those things that are important to him or her. Don't interrupt a good story because you think you must adhere to your outline. On the other hand, be sure to ask the questions that you think need to be addressed in the interview.

What kinds of questions should you ask? Use the reporter's "who, what, when, where, how, and why" method. The question, "Was Rev. Smith a good preacher?" may get a one-word response, but the question, "What was Rev. Smith's preaching style?" will give the narrator a chance to describe, interpret, and reminisce.

The narrator may not always have the facts straight. All of us get a little confused about dates and other details. Avoid confronting the narrator if you know what you are hearing is incorrect, unless it is absolutely critical to the story. It is the essence of the story that counts—the narrator's thoughts, feelings, reactions, impressions, interpretations, and analysis. Editorial corrections can be made in the typed transcript if necessary (for example, "The church burned down in 1971." [1972, ed.]).

Be careful not to bombard the narrator with too many questions all at once or with lengthy, rambling questions. Be brief and to the point! Remember that you are not the star of the interview. As long as your questions draw out the narrator, they do not have to be brilliantly phrased or eloquently delivered.

Relax! Don't worry about filling every moment with dialogue. Let the narrator pause to think about a response or to remember a detail. Your instinct may be to jump in with a question every time there are a few seconds of silence, but wait until you are sure the narrator is ready to move on.

Be sensitive to the narrator. If you sense that he or she is tiring, take a break. Ninety minutes is probably the maximum amount of time for an interview. If you feel there is more to talk about, arrange to meet another time. Choose a comfortable setting for the interview. Make sure that you have a pitcher of water and some tissues handy. Some people will be glad to come to the church or to your home, while others will be able to relax only in their own homes.

There may be times when the comfort level is so high that the narrator may say more than he or she intended. If the discussion becomes very personal and intimate, make sure the narrator remembers that the conversation is being recorded. Try to avoid "off the record" comments as much as possible.

After the Interview

Play the tape back immediately after the interview, so you can be sure that everything was properly recorded.

Write a thank-you note to the narrator, expressing your appreciation for his or her willingness to participate.

Audiotapes and videotapes have very short life spans. To preserve the information you have carefully recorded, do two things: copy the tapes every ten years, and create a typed transcript of the interview. Typing a transcript is a time-consuming process and requires accuracy and care. Be sure to have a third person read the transcriptions while listening to the tapes, just to make doubly sure the typed document is accurate.

Writing Your Church's History

Why Write a History?

• To tell the story of God at work in the life of your congregation.
• To gather and preserve the record of faithful witnesses through the years.
• To teach the members and friends of the congregation, now and in the future.
• To help your church see its ministry and mission as an ongoing pilgrimage.

Is It Time for a Church History?

When was your last church history written? If it was more than twenty-five years ago, it is probably time for an update. If you have no written history at all, it is certainly time to think seriously about writing one.

Are people in the congregation willing to work on this project? A good history is a collaboration of skilled researchers, writers, and editors. Each person must be enthusiastic, talented, and committed to the project. Even if the history is researched and written by one person, there should still be an editorial committee to support and oversee the project.

Will the church support the project? There must be money to print and promote a church history. Remember, too, that the project needs the approval and support of the pastors and other church leaders.

Starting the Task

The idea for writing a church history may come from the church historian or some other person or group. The church council (or similar body) should approve the project and its financing. It will be helpful if you prepare a detailed plan. Include a rationale for the project (why do we need a church history?), a time line for production and promotion, and suggestions for funding. Suggest what the final product will look like (how long, what format, and so forth). Looking at histories published by other churches may give you some good ideas.

The project should be assigned to the Committee on Records and History or to a special task force that includes representatives of all the major areas of church life.

Your history will be only as good as its author(s). You may want to select one or more persons in the congregation, or you may want to choose someone who is not a member of the church. If there are multiple authors, designate a chairperson or editor. The writer(s) should be guaranteed independence in judgment, but must be willing to listen to the counsel of a review board whose members will read and criticize the writing as it proceeds. Criticism (both positive and negative) is not easy for some writers to accept, but it is essential to writing a good history.

Develop a project budget that includes all fees and honoraria, mileage and telephone expenses, photocopying and supplies, publication and printing costs, publicity expenses, and the book's purchase price. Perhaps the best way to finance a history is to make the total cost a church budget item (over a three- or four-year period) so that one copy can be distributed to each church family. Sales will seldom cover the entire cost of a history. Funds may be raised by special contributions, or a single donor may provide the funds with the book dedicated to the donor or to someone the donor designates.

Conducting the Research
A number of persons can participate in the research process. Each can be assigned a specific topic (such as women's organizations, pastors' biographies, or architectural changes to the sanctuary). Anyone doing research must be dedicated to digging hard for as many facts as possible. It is up to the writer(s) to interpret those facts.

Sources of information include the church's records, conference journals and newspapers, and local newspapers. Work with the town librarian and the local historical society. Contact your annual conference archives and the General Commission on Archives and History. Examine every available source carefully. Evaluate it openly, and report the information fairly. To do less can result in an inaccurate and incomplete story.

Remember that you are writing for the future as well as the present: identify all persons, places, and events as accurately as possible. Check, recheck, and triplecheck facts and dates! People will rely on this history for many years to come.

Take care that all persons and groups are properly recognized for their role in the history of the church. The history should not simply document the clergy who have served your congregation.

Organizing the Story
The easiest way to organize a historical account is by chronological order: starting with the beginning and coming up to the present.

A second method is by periods, such as the early beginnings, a period of great growth, a controversial period; or on the basis of pastors who have served.

A third method is by topical arrangement. This basis offers more flexibility, but is more difficult to develop than the other two. A typical outline might look like this:

• Profile of the membership, past and present
• Organization of the congregation
• Buildings and other property
• Pastoral and lay leadership
• Organization and activities
• Worship and music
• Special occasions
• Service and mission
• Finances
• Ecumenical and community relations

No matter how you choose to organize your history, special touches can enrich the final product:

• Photographs enliven the text and provide another window to the past.
• Brief sketches about people and events add human interest to the story. Consider featuring these vignettes at the beginning of each chapter.
• Information about everyday things paints a picture of the times (the price of postage stamps, fashion trends, favorite radio programs). This helps the reader relate to the lives of historical figures.
• An index can be very helpful, and several appendixes may be useful (such as financial and membership statistics, lists of pastors, or names of church organizations in different eras). You may want to include a time line listing various milestones in the church's history.

Writing the Story

A good church history will faithfully record the past. It can also educate, entertain, and inspire. You want to tell the story of real people's lives, not tabulate dry statistics and lifeless facts. You want to reveal something of the depth, complexity, and texture of church life. Researchers, writers, and editors all need to remember that their goal is to put flesh on the bare bones of history.

It is very important to remember that your church's history has not happened in isolation. It has been a part of the community, both local and national. It has been affected by political events and social change. Its members have been concerned about the events of the world around them. Tell the story of your church in the context of its time and place.

Write clearly and concisely. Use brief, uncomplicated paragraphs. Place frequent subheads in the chapters to enable the reader to follow the account more easily. Don't use too many long quotations, which can interrupt the flow of the narrative.

Edit the rough draft carefully to ensure the accuracy of facts and interpretations and to strengthen style. Two or three drafts may be required as the committee provides editorial suggestions to the writer.

Publishing, Promoting, and Using the History

Discuss with your printer the appropriate way to prepare the copy, whether it is to be typeset or duplicated from your camera-ready copy.

Promote sales in advance, perhaps with a reduced prepublication price. Consider a special dedication service for releasing the history. Arrange for the writer(s) to be available to autograph copies. Provide a news story to local newspapers and your annual conference.

A church can use its published history in a variety of special ways. Encourage all members to read and study it carefully. Use it in membership orientation and confirmation training. Invite the writer to lead a special study on the church's history and to use the history as the basic text. A question that can be considered in various church groups is, What does our history tell us about our present responsibility, our future ministry, and our mission as a congregation?

Be sure to publish enough copies to provide an ample supply for a period of years. Arrange for safe storage and preservation of these extra copies. Present copies to your local library, the annual conference archives, and the General Commission on Archives and History.

Making History Come Alive!

One of your most important tasks is to encourage your church to recognize history and heritage as a part of its ministry. Learning about our heritage helps us learn about ourselves. Seeing how God has been at work in the past helps us see how God is at work in the present. Understanding where we have been helps us make decisions about where we need to go. How does history become a ministry? How can you share with the whole church family the good news of God's work in the church's past? There are as many ways as there are churches. What you decide to do will depend on your resources, your interests, and the help of others.

Observe significant anniversaries, whether your tenth or your hundredth. Plan events that will involve as many people as possible and that will bring history to life for young and old. Two resources published by the General Commission on Archives and History can help you: *Celebrating Our United Methodist Heritage: A Resource Packet for the Local Church* and *To Remember and Celebrate: Worship Resources for Heritage Events.* (See pages 29-30 for more information.)

Encourage church groups to celebrate their anniversaries. Your church library may be twenty years old or a choir or class may have been organized fifty years ago. Such celebrations can be tied to a Homecoming Sunday, where former members are invited to come back for worship and fellowship. Take photographs! This is also a time when an oral history project may be most appropriate.

Celebrate Heritage Sunday each year. Heritage Sunday is April 23 or the Sunday following. Heritage Sunday calls the church to remember the past by committing itself to the continuing call of God. The General Commission provides a theme and resources each year. Contact the General Commission and/or your annual conference Commission on Archives and History for information. A local church may also plan its own theme and program. Some congregations shift Heritage Sunday to fit their own schedule, sometimes moving it to a homecoming date in the summer. Certainly, your observance need not be limited to a worship service, but may include educational and fellowship opportunities.

Many historical projects can be done by the whole church or one of its organizations. Here are several suggestions:

• Prepare a list of the clergy from the United Methodist tradition who are buried in your church or area cemeteries, whether they served your congregation or not. Plan to mark their graves with the official United Methodist minister's grave marker, available from Cokesbury. Secure permission and have the markers installed by a qualified person. Conduct an appropriate service in the cemetery after careful research on the lives and times of the pastors. A suggested order of worship is included in *To Remember and Celebrate: Worship Resources for Heritage Events* (see page 29).
• Gather information about all the persons from your church who have entered full-time church vocations. Honor them with a special display and articles in your church newsletter or local newspaper. Add the information you have collected to the church archives so that it will be available to other researchers.
• When you discover bits of historical lore that are unusual, enlightening, dramatic, or funny, find a way to share them with the church family. Perhaps you can initiate a "History Minute" during Sunday morning worship, write a "Did You Know?" column in the church newsletter, or speak to Sunday school classes.
• Contact your annual conference Commission on Archives and History or the General Commission on Archives and History to learn what United Methodist historic sites or heritage landmarks are within a reasonable driving distance. Organize a tour with interested persons from your church.
• Alert your congregation to the historical activities of your annual conference and its Commission on Archives and History. Take other members with you to training events for historians. Get acquainted with the persons who can provide guidance and support, such as the conference historian or archivist.
• If your conference has a historical society, join it and encourage other members to join also. Enroll in the Historical Society of The United Methodist Church. Join your local historical society so that you can learn how your church's history connects to your community's history.

Resources

From the General Commission on Archives and History
P.O. Box 127, Madison, NJ 07940
Telephone: 973-408-3189
Fax: 973-408-3909
www.gcah.org

Historical Society Membership
Write for brochure. Basic membership includes a subscription to *Methodist History* (quarterly journal), *Historian's Digest* (society newsletter), and discounts on publications and other fees.

Methodist History
Official historical publication of The United Methodist Church, issued quarterly, containing articles on United Methodist events and personalities, book reviews, and analyses of trends across the years. Write for a brochure. Back issues are available, as are an index for volumes I-XX, 1962–1982, and an index for volumes XXI-XXXV, 1982–1997.

Archives and History Directory
Contains names and addresses of history leaders at the annual conference and general church levels. Also contains information about repositories and research centers. Loose-leaf format. Also available from our Web site.

Celebrating Our United Methodist Heritage: A Resource Packet for the Local Church
Contains four booklets: the *Planning Guide* identifies times and ways to celebrate and offers tips on organizing events, *A Songbook of Ideas* contains dozens of suggestions for celebrating history, *Voices from Our Past* is a collection of quotations from twenty important figures in United Methodist history, and the *Resource Directory* contains names and addresses that will be helpful to persons planning a heritage celebration.

Telling Their Stories: The History of Women in the Local Church
Resource packet with tips on oral history projects, exhibit design, and special programs for churches interested in recovering and celebrating the history of women in their own community. The packet includes a women's history time line and a suggested reading list.

To Remember and Celebrate: Worship Resources for Heritage Events
Contains suggested orders of worship and other resources for commemorating a church anniversary, Aldersgate Sunday, Heritage Sunday, installation of a gravemarker, consecration of a history room, and other worship experiences. The booklet also includes John Wesley's 1784 Order for Morning Prayer and Order for Administration of the Lord's Supper, suggested orders for worship in the nineteenth-century manner, and an order for a love feast.

Publications
Write for a current list and order blank for the numerous pamphlets and books on a variety of historical subjects. Titles include pocket-sized booklets on church founders and leaders, bibliographies, manuals, directories, and handbooks.

From Your Cokesbury Store, Mail Order, 800-672-1789

The Story of American Methodism, by Frederick A. Norwood.

United Methodism in America: A Compact History, edited by John G. McEllhenney.

United Methodist Studies: Basic Bibliographies, 1998 rev. ed., compiled and edited by Kenneth E. Rowe.

Sources for Archival Supplies

Conservation Resources International, Inc.
8000-H Forbes Place, Springfield, VA 22151
Telephone: 800-634-6932, 703-321-7730
Fax: 703-321-0629
www.conservationresources.com

Gaylord
P.O. Box 4901, Syracuse, NY 13221
Telephone: 800-634-6307
Fax: 800-272-3412
www.gaylord.com

The Hollinger Corporation
P.O. Box 8360, Fredericksburg, VA 22404
Telephone: 800-634-0491
Fax: 800-947-8814
E-mail: hollingercorp@erols.com

Light Impressions Corporation
P.O. Box 940, Rochester, NY 14603-0940
Telephone: 800-828-6216
Fax: 800-828-5539
www.lightimpressionsdirect.com

Metal Edge, Inc.
6340 Bandini Boulevard
Commerce, CA 90040
Telephone: 800-862-2228
Fax: 888-822-6937
Email: mtledge@1x.netcom.com

The Paige Company, Inc.
Parker Plaza, 400 Kelly Street, Fort Lee, NJ 07024
Telephone: 800-223-1901, 201-461-7800
Fax: 201-461-2677

University Products, Inc.
P.O. Box 101, 517 Main Street, Holyoke, MA 01041
Telephone: 800-628-1912; in Massachusetts, call 413-532-3372
Fax: 800-532-9281
www.universityproducts.com

The Book of Discipline is our book of covenant for The United Methodist Church. The following references in *The Book of Discipline,* 2000, relate to your task: 242, 246.5, 264, 530, 638, 1701-1712, 2545.5.